I0755972

FINISHING LINE PRESS
www.finishinglinepress.com

BREAK A PART

poems by

Laura Cesarco Eglin

Finishing Line Press
Georgetown, Kentucky

BREAK A PART

ISBN 979-8-89990-468-4 First Edition

ACKNOWLEDGMENTS

Thank you to the literary magazines that published some of the poems in this collection:

Ascendency: "Insomnia" and "I Make Room for Figuring Out"
Digo.Palabra.txt: "Hacia la lluvia"
The Elevation Review: "Coming to Terms"
MAYDAY: "Words of Collective Meaning"
Rejected Lit Magazine: "Breakup; Daybreak"

Thank you to Servane Briand for including my poems "Significance" and "The Atlantic Tides of My Language" in *Making Sense*, book 3 of the Passages of Babel Project.

Grateful to Joshua Gottlieb-Miller, Stalina Villarreal, Maria Miranda Maloney, and Elisa Garza-Leal for reading and giving love to some of the poems in this chapbook.

Publisher: Leah Huete de Maines
Editor: Christen Kincaid
Cover Art: Photo by author
Author Photo: Laura Lesta García
Cover Design: Elizabeth Maines McCleavy

Order online: www.finishinglinepress.com
also available on amazon.com

Author inquiries and mail orders:
Finishing Line Press
PO Box 1626
Georgetown, Kentucky 40324
USA

Contents

WHERE I LIVE

To write about realms instead of inhabiting them. Writing as a way to be involved. As magic involves the miraculous tentacles of translation. That is, discovery—discovery of desire. Like wanting to write something else. Like wanting to feel involved and in magic. Maybe that's what they mean by *in love,* because translation as discovery says something else about the miraculous, because the miraculous, like love, is a realm.

CODE SWITCHING

Sound out in this language
what encircles so much you
are glad to come closer
to your mouth
as it performs
reality;

what many times, every time,
is a different version
of slanted. A mouth
closing the distance
into possibilities.

OPTICAL ILLUSIONS

The trees marking a horizon
at the edge of the park. They play
at being nearby, but I know better.
As I walk toward them, distance
takes on a dimension: farther away.

I look to what's nearer me—
grasses reaching my knees.
Trees can have knees,
flexing and joining what I leave
behind and expectations.

LEARNING TO FEEL WITH THE WEATHER FORECAST

Cold can take a hold
of you in the most unlikely
of places. I feel it in my blue
nails that show me I should
keep warm. Temperature is only
what we acknowledge. I insist
I don't feel enough
cold. But I can't ignore the bold
body and its observations:
what it takes to feel
layers becoming more relevant
than a thermometer. Freezing
as in how I am doing,
as in where I have been. I keep
getting emails telling me to be
safe and ensure there isn't a burst
in the pipes. And yet sometimes
an outburst is more fitting than
ice melting into mud. The degrees
of what we allow to take hold
of us.

WHAT I REALLY WANT

I shouldn't have sent
the text. Reaching out as a form
of over-extending. A crush.
I shouldn't have gone looking
for a reaction as if I were a surfer
and needed a wave when the wave
knows so many words for falling and
I rage as the tumbling feels
rough—the coarse sand and the strength
of the water when I'm water in the water
and of the water is this fall and rise and I
refuse to stand even if the water is barely
waist high. Kicking and clawing I detonate
into pieces, which is what I wanted,
to crash from the start: break
to the point of no return, confuse
the shore with the horizon.

GROUNDBREAKING

Now you see me on the street. The pavement as backdrop. I'm what you'd call *discarded*. The lenses gone and I'm done with. But I want you to see the frame as what holds together and allows to focus and shift and reframe beyond the shapes and sizes. Stay here. Stay some time longer—enough to articulate the break. It breaks me when you don't know how to hold others with the shadows as part of perspective and frame.

BREAKUP; DAYBREAK

Parting with you is leaving
the butter outside the fridge
sitting on the dish. The blade
of the knife persistent
as it rests beside the rigid block.
The same kind of yellow
marks the beginning
of the day. As I go about without
you. Only in my mind—
knowing that I forgot
the butter, knowing nothing
will happen other than a softening
of the edges, and the sun
will merge into the sky. The rays
diffusing the blade of your absence.

OVER THE EDGE

A shattered glass is
the making of a plural and
the perfect excuse to think
what it means
to have an odd number
of glasses in your cupboard.
The gap between a cup
and a glass becomes large
like the spaces between
the fragments are larger
than absence.

A shattered glass is
not a nuisance
to be cleaned up.
Shards carry an edge
and the risk of losing
is all over the floor and I
am trying to notice
how each piece reconfigures
the story that started
in my hand and dropped
into a plot.

FEELINGS

What breaks and shatters
scatters to connect me
to what
I still don’t know how
to name
to feel

SIGNIFICANCE

I want to turn to Spanish as in
what I feel
I understand but am not certain
feel refers to a thought or if
it journeys the body. Somewhere
deep that can't be tied
to a particular organ.

Spanish turned into vital
as a connection
to meaning, yet it's not
clear *meaning* refers to *sense*
or *sentiment*—
how much feelings
signify into words.

I think it wards off leaving,
letting my language be
the cluster
that it is.

How language started out
as fate
and is destiny and now

HACIA LA LLUVIA

Ni una gota toca la ventana, como si no fuera vidrio, como si no fuera que me estoy empapando en frío, a mares. Hay algo quebrado. Ni una gota toca la ventana, como si la direccionalidad fuera más precisa de lo que entiendo, como si pudiera romper el vidrio, saber que está lloviendo. Quiero tocar lo que está realmente pasando. Ni una gota toca la ventana, como si no viera caer la lluvia, a cántaros, implacable. Romperme en llanto.

WORDS OF COLLECTIVE MEANING

Everything is intensified and wonder
as one more way to go
about the woods. Stay there
for a bit and a bite into the word
woods. How it wishes well
in one breath—the trees', regardless
of time, wind, and want.

Everything is intensified and wonder
into the particularities of forests
as opposed to trees and woods:
the difference in density and syllables
words are explicit about. The wonder,
bark, branch, and cone.

INSOMNIA

It’s 9 o’clock on a Monday and Tuesday
still seems far away. Breathing
for dreams
to help with deciphering
hours as a relative concept;
how long things last
as more
tangible. Understanding
through touch.

It’s 9 o’clock on a Monday and Tuesday
resembles more time—a blur when
one day and the next, entangled
for those that live the night as
nouns, like hours
and smaller divisions:
beginning, middle, or end.

I MAKE ROOM FOR FIGURING OUT

Pen to paper, like lies to lamp, or smile to symbolic.

Where does the moonlight shine through?

The phone doesn't ring for anyone. It calls
to itself.

I said I was a Leo, not a lion.

What would go into my autobiography
if not the milanesas I didn't have.

dislocation
fracture

What else is out of place?

The unexpected reality of absence.

Repetition of looking:

An image waiting for me to live in some form—
a blurring between the poem and the eye.

WHAT I LOOK FOR; WHAT I FIND

I was supposed to write about love
but all I can think about is how
when I looked at the clock
it was 1:01 but the word
palindrome doesn't apply
to numbers or love.

But I want to write
how special a time
like this is and how
I moved away from love
like 1:01 moved away
and it's already 1:05—

THROUGH WRITING

The quiet of the sand
as unsettling as everything
that moves and is
constant change. I
can't pinpoint a grain
until the wind blows through
my hair as it does through
the dunes, and *through* is always
more than from one side
to the next. *Through* is *around*
and *between* and *complete.* But not
utterly because I must

say words,
write them,
for the sand to have grains, for me
to care and find
quiet.

WHOSE VIEWPOINT POINTS THE VIEW

The lion's roar and what comes
out of my mouth. A monster
I love. When it's just us
we are comfortable and the pace
of together and inside carries me
to me and us and back.

But then I intersect with what
and who is outside. They
hear my words as
the other end of the night,
where the voices burst and bust.

They cover their ears to protect
from too much and I
return to my eyes.

COMING TO TERMS

Peeling a tangerine, slowly. Calling it *mandarina* because I need the extra syllable to take time, to touch the peel, feel it orange in my hands. Rip it apart. How different things are when we open them. How we do it. I look for another word that will lead me in without violence. Mandarina. Unfurl and release. To let go of force. Mandarina. Let the opening up happen of its own accord. Offer the hand. The rind on the plate, sometimes curling, sometimes many hints of what it used to be. A word as a contract with all its letters.

HOW I MAKE CHOICES

I chose the font because of its name.
Spinnaker: A guarantee for a journey.
It makes sense as I breathe
the word across the page.

The sea without land is ocean
and there is no sailing without
the spinnaker working with the wind.

Everything can't be in the foreground;
we lose direction if otherwise.

I can't decide what to call
the line: the spinnaker, the wind,
the journey, the sea—the font.

A broken line is not a segment
nor is it in pieces and defeated.

THE ATLANTIC TIDES OF MY LANGUAGE

The length of an afterward
that is pending: A look
at what's postponed
yet brought back
to mind, a call
to pay attention, back
and forth in constant flow
and ebb—how the directionality
of an expression can make you
forget the waves, the meaning of
spinning and tumbling without
having the repetition of breath
to translate the rhythm
straddling to keep us
here as there and there in here—
the perception—*at*
for location, for finding
oneself.

SEMANTICS

How can *dead end* be the right expression if I'm on it and thinking about it? More than death, there is hurt. Not on purpose. I am hurting—I stop the phrase there to prevent harm. But no intransitive mode will stop feelings from crossing over, going through, slashing up and down and sideways. Maybe the prefix *in* does not mean *without* but within, beside, inside.

ATTENTION TO DETAIL

What floats around in the morning. Suspended. You can call it dust but it's slower than that. It's a call to watch the verbs that linger after you see them. Suspend what you were doing. Read between the light, read between your sight. These universes, a whole story in those rays—inside your own house too! Traveling. Particles that you piece together like parts of a plot where everything happens simultaneously; together and so much. You sit and simply read the stories unfolding.

RETURNING THE HEART TO LANGUAGE AND LANGUAGE TO THE HEART

Sigh—only with intent
and release
the densities, reimagine
what it means to
undo the walls.
Sigh as language
to love
on the verge, the edge, the risk
to sigh so deeply your bones
become brittle and the tremor collates
with the only voice you can
muster. Sigh as if—
as if the edge of what is possible were
between the fog and the wind. Practice
the exhilaration of the about to
as epiphany opens up—suddenly and in miracle—
that smile. Sigh and there:
fog and wind. The language
of breathtaking

a beating heart

Laura Cesarco Eglin is a poet and translator from Uruguay. She is the author of six collections of poetry, including the chapbooks *Between Gone and Leaving—Home* (dancing girl press, 2023) and *Time/Tempo: The Idea of Breath* (PRESS 254, 2022). Her poems and translations (from the Spanish, Portuguese, Portuñol, and Galician), have appeared in many journals such as *Asymptote, Figure 1, Eleven Eleven, Puerto del Sol, Copper Nickel, Zócalo: Public Square, International Poetry Review, Tupelo Quarterly, Columbia Poetry Review, Timber*, and more. She is the translator of *claus* and *the scorpion* by the Galician author Lara Dopazo Ruibal (co•im•press, 2022), longlisted for both the 2023 PEN Award for Poetry in Translation and the 2023 National Translation Award in Poetry. Cesarco Eglin is also the translator of *Of Death. Minimal Odes* by the Brazilian author Hilda Hilst (co•im•press), winner of the 2019 Best Translated Book Award in Poetry. Her latest translations are *The Mistaken Place of Things* by the Mexican poet Gabriela Aguirre (Eulalia Books, 2024) and *Sardine* by the Galician poet Miriam Reyes (Ugly Duckling Presse, 2026). Cesarco Eglin is the publisher of Veliz Books.

www.ingramcontent.com/pod-product-compliance
Lightning Source LLC
LaVergne TN
LVHW090542110826
845146LV00003B/1225

* 9 7 9 8 8 9 9 9 0 4 6 8 4 *